KNIGHTS OF THE LUNCH TABLE

THE DRAGON PLAYERS

by
FRANK CAMMUSO

AN IMPRINT OF
■SCHOLASTIC

New York   Toronto   London   Auckland   Sydney   Mexico City   New Delhi   Hong Kong

For Khai
— FC

Special thanks to Ngoc Huynh, Hart Seely,
Tom Peyer, Susan Santola, Phil McAndrew,
Sheila Keenan, Phil Falco, David Saylor,
John Green, and David McCormick.

Library of Congress Cataloging-in-Publication Data

Cammuso, Frank.
The dragon players / by Frank Cammuso. — 1st ed.
p. cm. — (Knights of the lunch table ; 2)   "A Graphix chapter book."
Summary: Artie King and his Camelot Middle School friends, Percy
and Wayne, enter the annual Dragon Duel robot tournament to earn a
much-needed 300 dollars, then must decide whether or not to cheat.

ISBN-13: 978-0-439-90323-3 (pbk. : alk. paper)
ISBN-10: 0-439-90323-8 (pbk. : alk. paper)
1. Graphic novels. [1. Graphic novels. 2. Conduct of life – Fiction. 3. Contests – Fiction.
4. Middle schools – Fiction. 5. Schools – Fiction.] I. Title.

PZ7.7.C36Drd 2009   [Fic]--dc22   2008051463

10 9 8 7 6 5 4 3   09 10 11 12 13

First edition, September 2009

Edited by Sheila Keenan
Creative Director: David Saylor
Book design by Phil Falco
Lettering by John Green
Printed in the U.S.A.   40

YOU HAVE COME A LONG WAY, CHOSEN ONE.

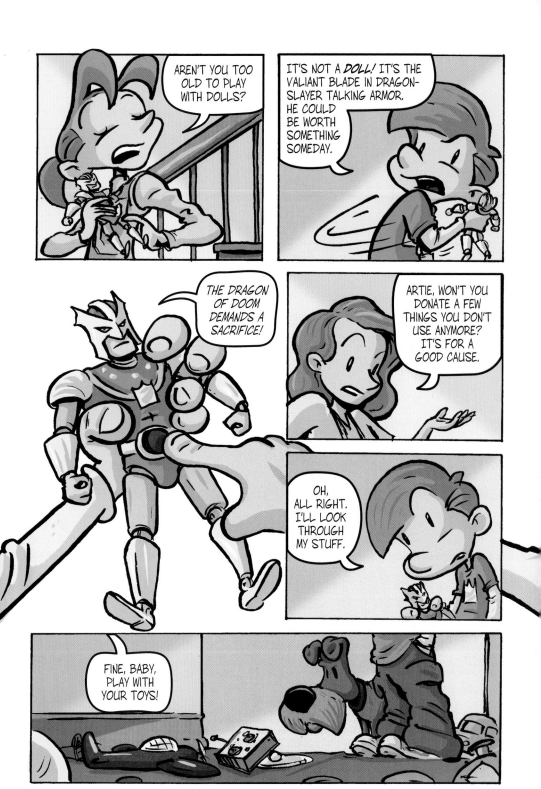

9

I'M SACRIFICING IT TO THE DRAGON DAY AUCTION. MY DAD WON'T MISS IT.

HAVE YOU SEEN PERCY? HE'S BEEN LATE ALL WEEK.

MR. ON-TIME? HMM, THAT'S NOT LIKE HIM.

WHAT'S NOT LIKE HIM?

DUDE, WHERE YOU BEEN?

YAWN! SORRY, I WAS UP LATE AGAIN.

WHY ARE WE OUT HERE?

WHERE'D YOU GET THAT?

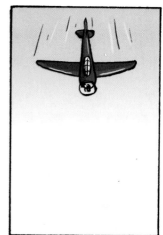

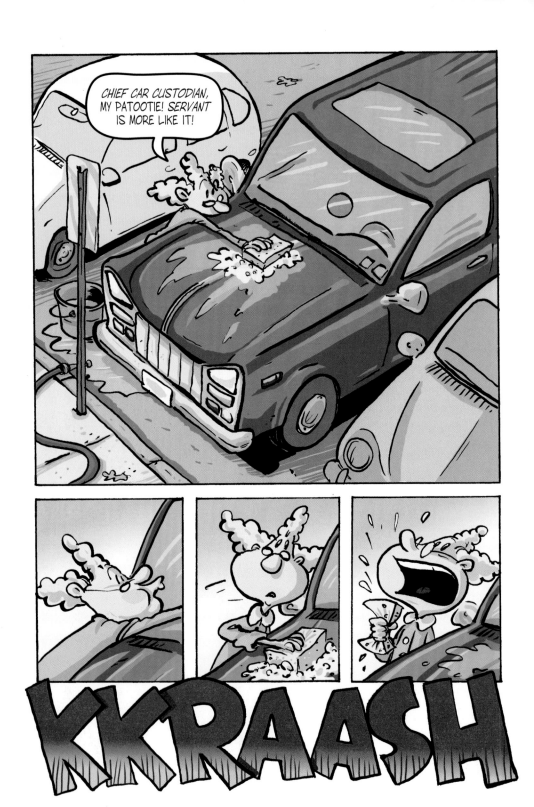

OH DEAR, OH DEAR, OH DEAR, OH DEAR.

WHOOOP·WHOOOP·WHOOOP·

WHOSE CAR ALARM IS THAT?

OF ALL THE OBNOXIOUS . . .

AAAAAAHHH!

SORRY, JOE, IT WAS AN ACCIDENT. HONEST.

REALLY? SORRY, BOYS, IT WAS AN ACCIDENT.

SNAP

HA HA HA.

IS THAT A SPIDER?

NICE TRY. I DON'T SCARE THAT EASY.

WHAT'S GOING ON?!

AAHHH!

SO WHAT DID THE GARAGE SAY, MISS FLUNKE?

THE SOONEST THEY CAN FIX YOUR WINDSHIELD IS *NEXT* TUESDAY.

NEXT TUESDAY?! I NEED MY WINDSHIELD FIXED *NOW!*

I MIGHT BE ABLE TO HELP.

MERLYN? DON'T YOU KNOCK? WHAT DO YOU WANT?

A FRIEND OF MINE OWNS A GARAGE. I'M SURE HE'D BE HAPPY TO REPLACE YOUR WINDSHIELD.

YOU HELP *ME?* WHAT'S THE CATCH?

NOTHING REALLY, JUST THE GOOD FEELING I GET FROM HELPING A FELLOW HUMAN BEING . . .

OH, AND I NEED TO BORROW YOUR GIGUNDO GAS-GUZZLER TO PICK UP AUCTION ITEMS FOR DRAGON DAY.

DRAGON DAY, YOU SAY?

IT WAS ONCE MY FAVORITE TIME OF YEAR, EVEN MORE BELOVED THAN FINAL EXAMS. DRAGON DAY: WHEN FEAR RULED AND THE STRONG PREYED UPON THE WEAK AND DEMANDED A SACRIFICE. I CALLED IT *DAGGER DAY.*

I ALMOST FORGOT HOW MUCH STUDENTS FEARED IT.

I STILL DO.

PEOPLE SAY THAT ON DRAGON EVE, A *DRAGON* ROAMS THE TOWN LOOKING FOR A SACRIFICE. IF YOU ARE OUTSIDE PAST DARK, HE WILL SWOOP DOWN AND TAKE YOU AWAY. JUST THINKING ABOUT IT GIVES ME THE CREEPS.

YES, WELL, DRAGON DAY HAS CHANGED FROM A DAY KIDS FEAR TO ONE THEY ENJOY.

IT IS STILL ABOUT SACRIFICE. THAT'S WHY WE'RE HAVING A CHARITY AUCTION. SO PEOPLE CAN DONATE SOME OF THEIR BELONGINGS TO A GOOD CAUSE. BUT IT'S ALSO ABOUT HAVING FUN AND LAUGHING AT WHAT MAKES YOU SCARED.

I DON'T KNOW WHAT YOU'RE UP TO, MERLYN, BUT THE ANSWER IS *NO!*

ABSOLUTELY NOT!

NEVER!

OK, HAVE IT YOUR WAY. HMM, ISN'T IT SUPPOSED TO RAIN TODAY?

OH, ALL RIGHT! YOU HAVE A DEAL!

BUT NOBODY DRIVES MY CAR BUT ME!

MISS FLUNKE AND I WILL PICK UP THE AUCTION ITEMS ON DRAGON'S EVE.

GULP

YOU DRIVE A HARD BARGAIN.

I'M DEAD. I'LL NEVER GET $300.

CHILL, WE'LL THINK OF SOMETHING.

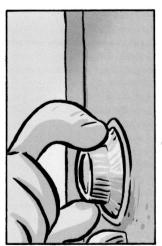

YOU NEVER KNOW WHAT WILL HAPPEN.

HEY, WHAT'S THIS?

CHECK IT OUT!

$300! THAT'S A NEW WINDSHIELD!

WHERE YOU GOING?

TO CLASS.

WE SHOULD DO THIS!

DUDE, IT'S A SIGN!

I DID FIND IT IN MY LOCKER.

IT'S NOT A SIGN. SOMEONE PROBABLY PUT THAT FLYER IN EVERY LOCKER.

IT'S A SIGN.

FOR THE LAST TIME: *THERE ARE NO SIGNS!*

WHAT ARE YOU POINTING AT?

DRAGON DUEL SIGN-UP HERE

DUDE, *THAT'S* A SIGN!

THERE'S NO POINT IN ENTERING. *THE HORDE* ARE THE REIGNING DRAGON DUEL CHAMPS.

THE HORDE? HOW'S THAT POSSIBLE?

THOSE MEATHEADS CAN'T PUT TOGETHER TWO WORDS, LET ALONE A ROBOT.

THEY CHEAT. EVERY YEAR, THE HORDE FORCES THE SMARTEST KID IN SCHOOL TO BUILD A ROBOT FOR THEM. THEY THREATEN TO SMASH THE KID'S STUFF OTHERWISE. JOE CALLS IT "THE SACRIFICE."

WE CAN BEAT THE HORDE. WE'RE THE *KNIGHTS!*

YEAH, WE BEAT THEM BEFORE . . . REMEMBER THAT LITTLE DODGE-BALL GAME, HMM?

YEAH, AND THEY'RE STILL MAD AND THEY'RE STILL BIG.

SO, WE—

WE CAN'T ENTER THE STUPID CONTEST! THE HORDE WILL CREAM US! UNDERSTAND?!

OK. SHEESH.

PERCY, ARE YOU...?

I GOTTA GO. WE'LL FIND ANOTHER WAY TO GET THE $300, WITHOUT GETTING CREAMED.

WHAT'S UP WITH HIM?

WHAT'S UP WITH WHO?

OH, HI, GWEN!

HI, GWEN.

BYE, GWEN.

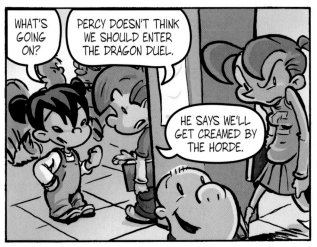

WHAT'S GOING ON?

PERCY DOESN'T THINK WE SHOULD ENTER THE DRAGON DUEL.

HE SAYS WE'LL GET CREAMED BY THE HORDE.

WELL, THEY *ARE* REIGNING CHAMPS.

YEAH, BUT WE NEED THE MONEY.

I HEARD ALL ABOUT THE TROUBLE WITH WAYNE'S DRAGON DAY OFFERING. BUMMER ABOUT THAT WINDSHIELD.

BUT THAT REMINDS ME: GOT ANYTHING ELSE YOU'D LIKE TO DONATE?

ARTHUR, KING OF MIDDLE SCHOOL, WITHIN THY HEART, TWO DRAGONS DUEL.

WHO SAID THAT?

OH, IT'S THEM AGAIN.

LADIES OF THE LUNCH? HELLO-O-O?

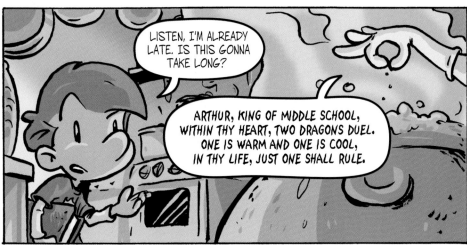
LISTEN, I'M ALREADY LATE. IS THIS GONNA TAKE LONG?

ARTHUR, KING OF MIDDLE SCHOOL, WITHIN THY HEART, TWO DRAGONS DUEL. ONE IS WARM AND ONE IS COOL, IN THY LIFE, JUST ONE SHALL RULE.

41

ARTHUR, WORK AND PLAY ARE OFTEN IN CONFLICT WITH EACH OTHER. YOU MUST CHOOSE WHAT'S MORE IMPORTANT.

SUCCESS IN SCHOOL MEANS MAKING THE RIGHT CHOICES.

CHOICES?

LET ME MAKE THIS EASIER. HAVE YOU THOUGHT ABOUT IMPROVING YOUR GRADE WITH EXTRA CREDIT?

WHAT KIND OF EXTRA CREDIT?

ENTER THE DRAGON DUEL.

THE ROBOT THINGY?

THE ROBOT THINGY. BUILD A ROBOT, WRITE A SCIENTIFIC DESCRIPTION OF IT, AND I'LL GIVE YOU EXTRA CREDIT.

DO I HAVE A CHOICE?

DEPENDS ON WHAT LEVEL YOU WANT TO BE STUCK AT.

45

BRAVO, ARTHUR. I'M GLAD YOU SIGNED UP FOR THE DRAGON DUEL!

WHAT?

MR. MERLYN, I...

I DIDN'T FORGET ABOUT THE EXTRA CREDIT.

EXTRA CREDIT?

I'M PROUD OF YOU. SOMETIMES IT TAKES COURAGE TO CHOOSE TO DO THE RIGHT THING. YOU'RE STANDING UP FOR WHAT YOU BELIEVE IN.

GEE, THANKS, BUT...

ENJOY YOUR LUNCH. I BELIEVE I HEAR SOME TATER TOTS CALLING MY NAME.

YOU'RE DOING EXTRA CREDIT?!

I THOUGHT YOU SIGNED UP TO HELP ME WIN THAT $300.

I DIDN'T SIGN UP!

I DON'T KNOW WHO WROTE IN MY NAME. BESIDES, WHAT'S THE PROBLEM?

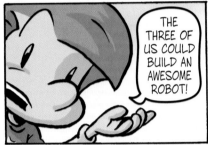

THE THREE OF US COULD BUILD AN AWESOME ROBOT!

YEAH, LET'S DO IT!

LET'S NOT!

WHY?

THE HORDE HAS ALREADY CHOSEN THE SACRIFICE.

BIG DEAL. WHY DO YOU CARE ABOUT THIS?

48

WHY DIDN'T YOU TELL US? ABOUT THE SACRIFICE, I MEAN.

IT HAPPENED BEFORE YOU MOVED HERE.

THE HORDE STOLE MY BIKE. THEY SAID IF I WANT TO SEE IT AGAIN, I'D HAVE TO HELP THEM.

WHY DON'T YOU GO TO MRS. DAGGER?

OH, RIGHT, SORRY.

MAYBE WE CAN GET YOUR BIKE BACK?

JUNKYA

JOE SAYS HE STASHED IT IN THE JUNKYARD.

THERE ARE TWO BIG KILLER DOGS IN THERE!

THAT'S WHAT I TRIED TO TELL YOU.

HEY, GEEKAZOID!

MY ROBOT DONE YET?

UH, NO.

I'VE BEEN STAYING UP LATE EVERY NIGHT BUILDING IT.

YOU BETTER BE. AND DON'T GET ANY IDEAS ABOUT HELPING YOUR DWEEBIE FRIENDS.

C'MON, GEEK, YOU GOT WORK TO DO.

STOP IT! YOU CAN'T DO THAT TO HIM!

DUDE, NICE ROOM! IS THAT THE VALIANT BLADE IN DRAGON-SLAYER ARMOR?

YEAH. HE TALKS, TOO.

DIE, FOUL BEAST!

YOU DO NOT KNOW HOW LUCKY YOU ARE NOT TO HAVE BROTHERS.

A SISTER IS NO TREAT.

WHERE DID I PUT THAT? I REMEMBER PACKING IT.

GRANTED. BUT YOU KNOW WHAT THE BIG DIFFERENCE IS?

WHAT?

NO ONE EXPECTS YOU TO SHARE A ROOM WITH YOUR SISTER.

THAT WOULD STINK. MORGAN IS ALWAYS TAKING MY STUFF.

ARDIS ROOM

WHAT ARE YOU LOOKING FOR?

MY CONSTRUCTION SET. THERE IT IS!

WE HAVE A ROBOT TO BUILD, REMEMBER?

U-BUILD-IT SET

OH, YEAH. YOU GOT ANYTHING TO EAT?

SURE, WHY?

I DO MY BEST WORK ON A FULL STOMACH.

I NEVER THOUGHT I'D SAY THIS, BUT I WISH PERCY WAS HERE.

HOW'S IT LOOK?

THIS ROBOT BUILDING IS A LOT OF WORK.

LET'S TEST IT OUT.

THIS BUTTON SHOULD MAKE IT MOVE FORWARD.

SPRONG!

CRASH

ARTIE! WHAT WAS THAT CRASH?

NOTHING, MOM!

DUDE, I GOTTA GO. SEE YOU TOMORROW.

MISS FLUNKE.

DID SHE ALREADY GO HOME?

MISS FLUNKE?

WHAT ARE YOU DOING?

UM, IT'S *DRAGON EVE*. I'D LIKE TO GET HOME BEFORE IT GETS DARK.

ARE YOU ACTUALLY *AFRAID* OF THE DRAGON SACRIFICE? THAT'S JUST A STUPID OLD FOLKTALE MEANT TO SCARE CHILDREN!

NO, MA'AM, IT'S TRUE. I'VE SEEN THE DRAGON MYSELF.

NONSENSE.

THE ONLY DRAGON THAT DEMANDS A SACRIFICE IS *ME*.

BESIDES, YOU HAVE TO HELP ME PICK UP ITEMS FOR MERLYN'S AUCTION.

BUT, BUT . . .

NO BUTS, GLADYS. *THIS* DRAGON DEMANDS HER SACRIFICE.

LISTEN, WARTIE, WHEN YOU GET HOME TODAY, TELL MOM SHE DOESN'T HAVE TO DROP OFF THE AUCTION STUFF . . .

ARTIE! CONGRATS!

OH, HEY, GWEN . . . CONGRATS ON WHAT?

BECAUSE YOU SIGNED UP FOR THE DRAGON DUEL, TWO MORE TEAMS ENTERED THE CONTEST.

YOU'RE AN INSPIRATION TO THEM.

WOW, REALLY?

SO, HOW'S YOUR ROBOT COMING?

NOT SO GOOD.

ARTIE, WAYNE, WAIT UP!

HOW'S YOUR ROBOT COMING?

TERRIBLE. WE COULD USE YOUR HELP.

I CAN'T; NOT WHILE THE HORDE HAS MY BIKE.

TOO BAD YOU CAN'T ASK YOUR MAGIC LOCKER FOR HELP.

THAT'S IT!

DUDE, WHERE YOU GOING?

HIS NAME, *E-V-O*, IS STILL TOP SCORE ON HALF THE STINKIN' GAMES.

REALLY? WHAT HAPPENED TO HIM?

HE BEAT EVERY GAME BUT ONE: *INTERNAL WAR*. HE JUST COULDN'T GET TO THE FINAL LEVEL. HE GOT MAD AND STARTED POUNDING ON THE MACHINE. WE HAD TO BANISH HIM FROM ARCADIA.

SO HOW CAN EVO HELP US?

WELL, WE DISCOVERED EVO DIDN'T BEAT THE GAMES WITH QUICK REFLEXES. HE WAS SOME KIND OF EVIL TECHNOWIZARD. HE CONSTRUCTED A DEVICE TO *CHEAT* THE GAMES.

WHERE DO WE FIND HIM?

MAYBE YOU GUYS SHOULD LEAVE HIM ALONE. EVO IS . . . *WEIRD*.

WE'VE NO PLACE ELSE TO TURN.

OKAY, BUT IF I TELL YOU, PROMISE ME YOU'LL BE CAREFUL. HE LIVES AT . . .

...27 TOWER TERRACE, THIS IS IT.

MAYBE WE SHOULDN'T DO THIS?

THIS NEIGHBORHOOD IS WEIRD.

SCOTT SAID EVO IS AN EVIL TECHNOWIZARD.

SINCE WHEN DO EVIL WIZARDS HAVE GARDEN GNOMES?

A GARDEN GNOME!

THE LUNCH LADIES TOLD ME TO BEWARE THE GNOME.

LUNCH LADIES? GARDEN GNOMES?

DUDE, WE'RE HERE. LET'S AT LEAST ASK.

DING DONG

CLICK CLICK KLAK

HELLO, MAY I HELP YOU?

YES, HELLO, MA'AM. WE'RE LOOKING FOR A FELLOW NAMED EVO?

NOBODY HERE BY THAT NAME. I LIVE HERE WITH MY BOY, EDDIE.

SORRY, MA'AM.

NOW WHAT?

LET'S GO HOME.

GREETINGS, TRAVELERS.

AHH!!! EVIL GNOME!

PUT THAT DOWN! IT'S NOT A TOY!

SORRY, I . . .

THIS IS A *COLLECTIBLE!* I POSSESS NEARLY THE FULL SERIES.

I LACK ONLY ONE, THE VALIANT BLADE IN DRAGON-SLAYER TALKING ARMOR.

I HAVE THAT ONE. IT WAS A BIRTHDAY GIFT.

LIAR! ONLY 27 WERE MADE.

IF YOU CAME HERE TO TAUNT ME, YOU CAN LEAVE!

BUT WE NEED YOUR HELP WITH THE DRAGON DUEL.

THE DRAGON DUEL? DID YOU KNOW THAT I—EVO—WAS THE FIRST CHAMPION OF THE DUEL?

REALLY?

YES, SEE?

WOW.

COULD YOU HELP US WIN?

NEVER! EVO DOES NOT HELP CHILDREN!

BUT PERHAPS IF YOU WERE TO SACRIFICE A CERTAIN ACTION FIGURE.

IN YOUR DREAMS.

HAVE IT YOUR WAY. ENJOY THE BITTER TASTE OF . . .

IF I GIVE YOU THE ACTION FIGURE, WILL YOU BUILD US A ROBOT?

EVO DOES BUILD ROBOTS, BUT . . .

I WILL CRAFT YOU A DEVICE THAT WILL *GUARANTEE* YOUR VICTORY.

OK, DEAL. MY VALIANT BLADE IN DRAGON-SLAYER TALKING ARMOR FOR YOUR HELP.

SPLENDID. I'LL NEED SUPPLIES. BRING ME A REMOTE CONTROL DEVICE FOR COMPONENTS.

WHERE DO WE GET THAT?

NOT MY PROBLEM.

WHEN DO I RECEIVE MY TOY?

IT'S NOT A TOY, IT'S A COLLECTIBLE.

ARTIE'S HOUSE

KING

EXCUSE ME, COMING THROUGH!

YOU LITTLE JERK!

HERE YOU GO, MRS. DAGGER.

THANK YOU, CHILD, PUT IT IN THE BACKSEAT.

THE JUNKYARD

PERCY?

GRRRRRR!

HOLD ON, I'M THINKING.

I DON'T THINK THE DOGS LIKED THE COOKIES.

GRRRRRRR!

RWAAK! RED HOT!

BATH TIME, DOGGIES!

88

92

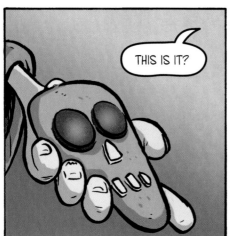

HEY, MR. MERLYN.

ARTHUR, YOU SEEM CHIPPER TODAY.

I FEEL LIKE A WINNER!

NOTHING WRONG WITH A LITTLE CONFIDENCE. TOO MUCH IS A DIFFERENT . . .

RWAWK! EEE-VOOH!

WHAT'D HE SAY?

PAY NO ATTENTION TO OBERON.

NO, I WANT TO KNOW.

IT HAPPENED A LONG TIME AGO. BUT, IF YOU'RE INTERESTED . . .

A FEW YEARS BACK, I HAD A BRILLIANT STUDENT NAMED EDWARD VORTIGERN. KIDS NICKNAMED HIM EVO.

EVO?!

YOU KNOW EDWARD?

UH, NO, GO ON.

EDWARD WAS A STRAIGHT-A STUDENT. HE EXCELLED AT ALL THINGS ACADEMIC. HE NEEDED TO BE THE BEST AT EVERYTHING AND HE HATED COMPETITION.

SO, WHEN HE ENTERED THE FIRST-EVER DRAGON DUEL, EDWARD'S ROBOT EASILY WON.

WHERE DID I PUT THE MEALWORMS?

THEY WERE HERE YESTERDAY.

RWAWK! CLOSET!!

THAT'S RIGHT. THANKS, OBERON.

WHAT ABOUT EVO?

YES, WELL, EDWARD'S DRAGON DUEL VICTORY CAME AS NO SURPRISE—THAT IS UNTIL WE FOUND OUT *HOW* HE WON. HE CHEATED.

WHAT?

IS SOMETHING WRONG, ARTHUR?

UM, NO. I'M OK. HOW DID EVO CHEAT?

HE USED A REMOTE CONTROL TO SHUT DOWN THE OTHER PLAYERS' ROBOTS.

THAT'S PRETTY CLEVER.

YES, AND IT'S ALSO PRETTY AGAINST THE RULES.

SO WHAT HAPPENED?

EDWARD WAS STRIPPED OF HIS PRIZE.

WHY DO YOU THINK HE DID IT?

WHO KNOWS? BUT I CAN TELL YOU THAT, LIKE EVERYONE, EDWARD HAD TWO DRAGONS FIGHTING INSIDE HIM.

TWO DRAGONS?

SURE. ONE STANDS FOR WHAT'S RIGHT: SHARING, KINDNESS, COMPASSION, AND TRUTH. THE OTHER STANDS FOR ALL THE BAD STUFF LIKE FEAR, ANGER, GREED, AND DECEIT. AND THOSE DRAGONS ARE ALWAYS FIGHTING.

SO WHICH DRAGON WINS?

THE ONE YOU FEED THE MOST.

SOMETHING WRONG, ARTHUR?

NO, I THINK I FORGOT TO FEED MY DRAGON.

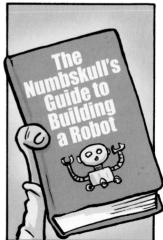

DRAGON DAY

CAN'T WE GET SOMETHING TO EAT, THEN FIND ARTIE?

PIZZA - SAUSAGE

THERE HE IS OVER THERE.

WAK -A- WYRM

DUDE, WHAT'S UP?

RULES

OH, HEY.

SOMETHING WRONG?

NO, JUST THINKING ABOUT DUELING DRAGONS.

DUDE, DON'T WORRY, WE ARE GOING TO *DEVOUR* THE HORDE. SPEAKING OF WHICH, I'M STARVING.

MMMM, ARE THOSE CHICKEN WINGS?

TODAY THEY'RE CALLED *DRAGON WINGS.*

MR. MERLYN!

GLAD YOU BOYS COULD MAKE IT! READY FOR THE DRAGON DUEL?

I GUESS.

WE'VE GOT A SECRET WEAPON!

SECRET WEAPON, HUH? SAY NO MORE. I UNDERSTAND IT'S CONFIDENTIAL. GOOD LUCK, FELLOWS, SEE YOU AT THE DUEL.

YOU'VE GOT SUCH A BIG MOUTH!

WHAT'D I SAY?

WAYNE, WE'RE NOT GUARANTEED TO WIN.

NONE OF YOUR BUSINESS.

ARTIE?

ROD OF WRATH.

WHO'S ROD O'RATH?

IT'S NOT A *WHO*, IT'S A *WHAT*.

THE *ROD OF WRATH* IS A DEVICE THAT CAN TURN OFF ANY OTHER ELECTRIC DEVICE.

SO WE CAN TURN OFF THE HORDE'S DRAGON. HOW COOL IS THAT?

THAT'S CHEATING!

SO? THE HORDE CHEATS!

THEY STOLE MY BIKE AND MADE ME BUILD THEIR DRAGON.

THE HORDE DOES CHEAT.

WHAT'S WRONG WITH CHEATING THE CHEATERS?

ONLY THAT THEN *WE'D* BE THE CHEATERS.

IF THEY HAD IT, THE HORDE WOULD USE THE ROD OF WRATH ON US.

YOU'RE RIGHT. THE HORDE *WOULD* USE IT ON US.

SEE.

THAT'S WHY WE CAN'T USE IT ON THEM.

WHAT?!

109

Dragon Wings

STEP ASIDE, THE WARRIORS ARE HUNGRY.

HEY, MOM! MORGAN.

HEY, GUYS!

WHAT DO YOU TWO DWEEBS WANT?

WHERE'S THE REST OF THE GANG?

THEY'RE GETTING OUR ROBOT READY.

WHAT CAN I GET YOU BRAVE WARRIORS?

WINGS, PLEASE.

HOW DO YOU LIKE THEM? MILD? HOT? OR DRAGON HOT?

LISTEN, JOE, I'VE GOT A SURPRISE FOR YOU.

IT BETTER BE SOMETHING TO EAT, 'CAUSE I'M STARVING!

HEH HEH, IT'S BETTER THAN FOOD. I'LL GO GET IT!

WELL, WHERE IS IT?

I DUNNO, IT WAS HERE A SECOND AGO.

FORGET ABOUT IT. I'M HUNGRY. GET ME SOMETHING TO EAT.

I DON'T HAVE ANY MONEY.

DOES IT LOOK LIKE I CARE?

LADIES AND GENTLEMEN, WELCOME TO THE 9TH ANNUAL DRAGON DUEL.

I CAN'T BELIEVE IT!

WHAT?

SOMEONE STOLE MY WINGS.

WE'LL GET MORE LATER. COME ON, THE DUEL IS STARTING.

OUR FIRST DRAGON TONIGHT COMES FROM THE REIGNING CHAMPS, THE HORDE.

PLEASE WELCOME *THE DESTRUCTINATOR!*

GEE, PERCY, NICE DRAGON YOU BUILT THEM!

THANKS.

117

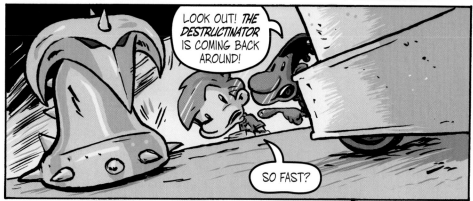

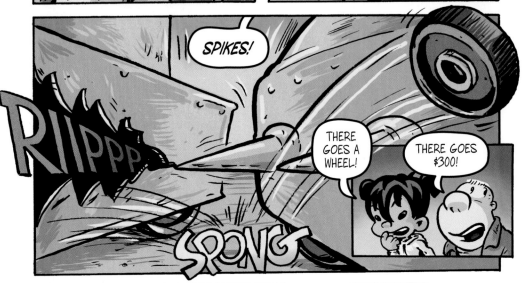

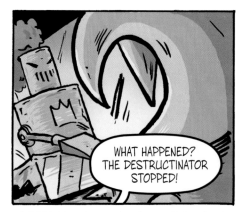

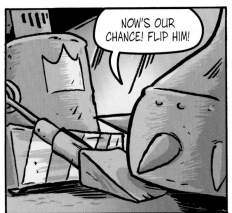

124

DING

DONG

Dragon Duel master Frank Cammuso is a three-time recipient of the Wedgie. He has also received the prestigious Noogie and the Hurtz Donut.

Cammuso wrote and drew *Knights of the Lunch Table: The Dodgeball Chronicles*. He is also the Eisner-nominated creator of the Max Hamm, Fairy Tale Detective graphic novels. He draws political cartoons for the *Post-Standard* and his work has appeared in *Newsweek*, the *New York Times*, the *Washington Post*, and *USA Today*. He lives with his family in Syracuse, New York.